Poetic Licence

Mike Alfred

Botsotso Publishing

First published in 2007 by Botsotso Publishing
Box 30952 Braamfontein, 2017, South Africa
email: botsotso@artslink.co.za
website: www.botsotso.org.za

ISBN 978-0-620-38520-6

We thank the following funders for their support:

Editor: Allan Kolski Horwitz

Cover and text design & Layout
Anna Anuradha Varney

Acknowledgements: Botsotso, Carapace, Kotaz, New Coin,
New Contrast, Southern Rain.

To Cecily, my pillar of support and loyalty –
for these 44 years...

Contents

34 Collingwood St

Once the stream was not
a gutter; when water dribbled
from moss between stones.
Once the river was not a
culvert; when antelope drank
at dusk and lions coughed on
whiteswept mornings. Once, no
iron roofs, ringing in the sun,
no bar brawls or litter, no exotic
forest with Loeries and Barbets.

But the koppies remain geological,
Sandstone and Banket, chocking
our eyes with time. The same wind
blows, carrying the scent of elephant,
which we don't recognise. Mists erase
the city. Thunder, hail and lightning
thrash the slopes. The sky we know
surrounds the world, and lizards
lounge forever.

A small biography...

and a short history
of a little fathering
and a little business
and a little poetry
and a little more than a little loving
and a little more wine thank you
and twenty three pairs of walking shoes
and much talk
and much thought
and a little action
and a little…
and a…
and…

A few didactic intimations from the Master of the Universe

I can, said the creator, I can
offer, he said, only a life. Just
the spark to the starter motor,
a puff, a squeak and I'm done.
Life is all I can give you. Haven't
you realised that I'm an experimenter,
not an insurance salesman? So you
see, survival, survival is up to you;
it's your adventure. I can't guarantee
silk stockings, an apartment in Manhattan,
or pure intentions. But here's a word of
advice: don't put too much store in the words of
politicianseconomistsparentsteachersbossesexpertsbureaucratsmarketers,
they're purveyors of an obscene accumulation of
useless cant. And yes, if you press me, the
churches as well; far too powerful,
stronger than I. Isn't that something
now, stronger than god? Knocks all
your beliefs sideways doesn't it?
Sometimes I think I should have
become more directly involved.
Trouble is, I'm not all that sold on
morality. And anyway, running a
universe is one hell of a task. So as
I said, when the sperm docks with
the ovum, [hey, how's the space
age imagery?] my role is over.
My work ended when I got this evolution
thing working smoothly, well, more or less.
Allowed me to start tinkering with

other problems. There we are then,
that's my part of the deal: your life. And
there's one big advantage let me tell you,
you don't have to sign anything.

At the Party

At the party, a psychologist
mesmerised me with tales of hypnotherapy.
I couldn't stop asking damn fool questions.
A guest declared his hundred thousand rand
flight into the Alaskan wilds to fish.
To fish? To fish!

As our escape routes coincided, an Irish brogue
told me about his fulfilled life, marred only
by his residential proximity to Soweto.
A clairvoyant insisted she saw my long dead
mother hovering at my shoulder. I fled to the
garden.

When I returned unseen, the fisherman was
entrancing the clairvoyant who solemnly
predicted the passage of time. Mother refused
the Irishman's invitation to dance. The psychologist
was practising group therapy. My hostess looked
as glazed as her ham.

My wife heard an owl hooting
in the pines. The guard discovered fairies at the
bottom of the garden. South Africa, breathing heavily
at the window, wished me a confusion of Xmas. I
remembered the relief of Ladysmith

An anxious note to Tar Bomb Becky

Friends tell me, you're not too fond of ah, ah, you know,
those people.
Oh dear, is that really true?
May I remind you of all the nice things
we've done for you recently!

Hello, helloo.

Well, I suppose we had to hear it sooner or later?
After all, this is a democracy, with all its freedoms.
I mean, you can speak out now!
You certainly have that right.
I mean, no one will introduce you to Robben Island.

Do you really dislike us?
Perhaps it's just a vague uneasiness?
Perhaps it's just politics, playing to the gallery, hey?
Perhaps you dislike only some of us?
Not the nice ones, like ah, someone we could name, if
pressed.
Some politicians have been known to work their supporters
into a frenzy.
You wouldn't do that would you?

I hope you're just having a little fun?
Wagging a playful finger like, so we behave ourselves,
learn Sikilele.
In the meantime, we'll just have to get on with our lives,
won't we,
now that we've become the minority we always were?

This cat...

is not zoology.
She's the one
sitting next to Queen
Nefertiti, ruling the kingdom.
She insists on wearing this
raggedy, cat-fur jacket.
She thinks I'm one of the
goodies from Star Wars.
She leaps upon me,
we rub noses,
"Adore me!" she demands.
"I'm hungry, you've been away
a long time," she scolds.
Occasionally she goes moggy.
Off we go for hormones,
    complaining all the
            way down
                the hill
                    to the
                        vet.
"What did you do before people?"
She knows when to keep silent.
She knock-kneed bustles down
the passage in her straggly coat.
Give her a brief-case and
she'll rid the country of crime.
She mocks Man the superior. She'll
be around long after we're gone.
She thinks she's a braille
alphabet or a love-violin.

On the day after

During the drought,
on the day after the day
of rain, Emmarentia was
singing, humming, whistling,
waving, dancing drunk. On the
day after, it was flowing, rushing,
gurgling, splashing, wringing wet.
And the smiling dogs knew and their
people nodded and grinned and talked,
and the tremulous roses blazed away.
The po-faced geese and coots pedalled
crazily through the rising waters.

Sluiced and shining, the trees hugged
the humid ghosts on the morning after
the day of rain.

Phoenix Sinking

Two waiters, I can bring to mind.
One with the mythic thumb; the
digit awash in the generous plate of
free soup. Thumb soup we called it.
We'll have some thumb soup. His
pop-eye face reacted not. We
received a spoon-proof wash on the
bottom of our plates. No more smart eh?!,
he didn't need to say. The other, tall,
lady-killer rough, with slicked black
hair in Brylcream. Maestros, they
manouevred farmfulls of foaming
tankards with never a slopped drop.
Neither was friendly. Nothing part-time
about those two; no Ph.d in the wings,
no waiting for better things. Serving table
was their life's grind or pleasure, who
could measure? Tips disappeared
without a flicker.

The Phoenix, down becoming
tatty, Bree St., next to the tombstone
place, where dad bought me my first
dose of dark German draught, a
schoolboy's rite of passage. It was
a soup of the yesterday place, an
eisbein place, a generous goulash
place, a plateful of dumplings place, a
fried potatoes and onions place,
where wurst and sauerkraut crept
up and around nasal passages. We ate

warm and winter-fuggy, or cool under
the backyard, summer vines.
Cheap it was, and Bisto-bathed, luring
the blessed and short alike, students,
young marrieds with their unimpressed
first bawl, ties-askew businessmen,
sloshed journalists in beer mat frisbee
wars. Showpeople: Bill the booming anecdote,
of the mutton-chop whiskers and the pork chop
appetite, he expounded there, expanded there.
Bachelors in their comfort-clasp, studying
anew the well-remembered, soup-splashed
menu at proprietary tables, under old black &
whites of trams in Eloff St.

It was a dropping-in, sharing tables
place, a no pretensions place, a
many-roomed, mixed-grill place, a Joeys
constant, as comfortable as worn-in shoes,
as reliable as French trains.

Suddenly, it was torn down for progress, one
day here, next day gone. All that contentment,
those memories and fun, all those plates
of soup, tipped into a rubbled hole.

Progress didn't win; resurrection
and transplant, together too traumatic.
Phoenix two in Jeppe St., turned
belly-up without jackhammer's help.

Surfing Crows

Crows know about air;
all there is to know. Maybe
they don't know they know,
but they do. Every bone, muscle
and feather has attended flight
training since the outbreak of
evolution. Up stream, down cliff,
over tundra and desert, they
are at one with air. They'd be
the last to discover it.

How they love the north
wind that builds a scaffold
on Langermann Kop. When
that north wind ripples their
feathers, they tremble with
anticipation, they smile and
chuckle, flex their wings,
report sick.

North wind days are
hanging motionless days.
North wind days are balancing
days; they're for gravity-defying
games. North wind days are
surfing days, holidays,
without wingbeat,
lazy days.

They straddle the updraught, with
full flaps and undercarriage down.
Without losing altitude, just hanging,
they allow the wind to win, centimetre
by centimetre, until, banking suddenly,
they slice the wave, race down the crest,
flip out, climb back to
do it again and
again and
again.

Schizo

In the words of that wonderful song:
I never thought I'd come to this;
spindoctoring for the city, conspiring
to gloss another powerless night,
another waterless day, another billing fiasco,
another traffic jam, more filth in the streets,
another corrupt policeman, another incompetent
bureaucrat, and another deaf;
conniving to ignore more slumlords,
more druglords, more beggars,
more Aids orphans.
It's a long list.

I'm becoming the marketing personality
I love to hate, pushing the product,
waxing grandiloquent for good old Jozi,
fashioning new myths, using my
lense selectively, playing dreamy music,
using the old 'voice over,' aiming
Nelson's eye at the evidence,
driving home in my
four by four.

Dying Crow

Those crows who
know about air, that
small family who surf
the updraughts on
Langermann Kop, who
kraak kraak above my
house, who nest in the
tallest bluegum at
Rhodes Park, those
alchemistic totems,
those venerable ancients,
even they, are not
immortal.

On my walk I found him
sitting on the soccer field,
forlorn, blind and feeble,
unable to fly another step.

I sat down beside him to
say goodbye: goodbye my
surfing crow. He stirred
slightly. His relations
yelled at me from the tree.

When next I walked
there, his dry remains,
a mix of bones, skin
and feathers, lay stretched
upon the grass.

Slovo's Short Freedom

Were those his best times,
walking alone in the sun
with his be-ribboned spaniel?
Walking again in the sun of
his youth, in the nostalgic
sun of his exile, and now
the glowing sun of fulfilment.
Basking in the warm space
of victory, under the blue Highveld
sky, old Johannesburg solid
wherever he looked. Home at
last, bearing the living hopes
of the dead and the dead
hopes of the living.

Yes, I think those were his
best times; before bodyguards,
before the elections, before the
clarion's demands wrung the
strength from his already
invaded frame. When he rejoiced
on sunny afternoons in Bez
Park, strolling, smiling at
strangers like me, snatching
those few warm minutes before
assuming the hopes of the
dead and the barely living.

We live in a low…

We live in a low orbit
ship called Joey White.
Our hand seldom strays
from the booster lever,
or the bag of numismatic
memorials. We bling past
the masses, wondering
who will save us if we land?
We're dab hands at should be:
should be cleaner, should be safer,
stricter, incorruptible, etcetera.
We dally with London and
Auckland but settle for Provence
with Electronic Devices and The Berg.
We ponder being African, but cannot
betray our culture. We smile too much
and try too hard and talk as if we're
being monitored. The longer we stay,
the richer we become; surely that's
a form of commitment?

Now and then

In Hillbrow then, I walked
alone, afar and safe. For
Mummy's sixty cigs a day;
to the playground in the
park; for barber de Jongh's
short back and sides and
Comic Cuts. I met Dick
Tracy in the sixpennies
at Art Deco Clarendon.
Hillbrow, my Uhuru.

Now a child might be more
careful. 'Don't buy a thing
from the Nigerians. Don't
walk alone after dark.' But
she'd read the pimps and
prostitutes, count the Volvos
for the Summit Club, dodge
the lurchers; she'd learn
which side to walk on,
at whom to smile.

Later the physician will
recall 'skin and bone, skin
and bone.' 'I was always
ducking thro' dark spaces,'
is the architect's clerestory.
'That stink!' that's what
enchanted the City Engineer.
The social worker wept
for streetkids. After she'd
stopped running.

The druglord, now living with
two poodles, in a far off place,
children at good schools, he
can't remember, 'No, I can't
remember; who, where
when? No, no, not there!'
Uhuru dons a pain, a pose,
Hillbrow, just a place in the
horrified mind.

Ah Joburg

you golden skinflint capitalist bastion
you hide behind fences and turncoats with guns
you herd us into the seedier parts of town
you curse the cardboard shanties over our heads
you sell us clapped out smoking motor cars
you mouth the great psalm of black empowerment
we're sick and tired of Patrice Motsepe TV
you close your eyes and prattle about collateral
you chase our traders off the streets
you provide no transport

and still we smile and
beg to mow your lawns
beg to clean your toilets
while you look past us

oh yes we saunter in front of your BMWs
piss in your parks and strew them with rubbish
yes when we're not aching with smile we stare at you
we dice and weave and hoot you when the light turns yellow
and we taunt your policemen and turn your officials into
collaborators
and we beg and steal and sell drugs and prostitute ourselves
forgive us please for raising capital and gleaning influence
do you teach only survival
good man, smiling widely
as we guard your cars

Ah Joburg
cultivar of consumerism
exemplar of envy

show us a job
better
show us a career
something to make life meaningful
you focus our minds so sharply
you're one merciless bastard
of a mentor

Norwood

Norwood's a street up
to no good. Just driving
by, you can tell. All that
red line, coffee-royalty,
dressing dark, driving
fancy, wearing facelift
sex. Their eyes keep
slipping and sliding.
All those restauranteurs
who can't cook or pour
a drink. Israelis put
their boots in
chairs and look you
leather. Norwood's
an all-day, in-your-face,
while good people are
earning their livings
somewhere else.
Norwood's wearing
a steely glint called
smile.

Meeting the Organism

His body parts are filing grievances.
His double helix is cursing the family history.
'Marketing Man of the Year' trips over his liver.
Discussing plumbing with his cardiologist, his
friend, the 'top legal expert,' discovers his heart.
His organs start dating green-gowned gods.
Mother Nature sends flowers, but they're for everyone.
Tumours show no respect for his renowned indignation.
His ego can no longer win the game of doubts.
God is abandoned for anatomy and physiology.
Having been greater than the sum of his parts,
he enters the precocious realm of deconstruction

I saw a man

I saw a man sitting
in the sun on the curb,
crutches alongside,
resting his bare feet,
taking a break from work.

I can think of no harder work:
a thousand daily rejections,
fifty cents per smile.

God is evolving...

no longer a moon, a fiery chariot,
no longer a stag, a Pantheon or
sleight-of-hand.
He wonders how he begat a son?
God is rendered more mysterious
by science, more invisible by dogma.
He watches us in dumbstruck
amazement; his name a lending
library, a martial banner. He enjoys
our religious architecture. [He's the
one with the telephoto lens.] God is
ineffable, even unto himself. He can
meditate for a million years.
Sometimes the universe is too fast
for him. At his poker school no one
wins all the time. God is Philosophy
honours. God is breathless. Little
by little, God unfolds himself,
amazed at what emerges.

Themeda Finale*

There's a place on earth, up
the pass, alongside plantations,
swaying through mud in rain.
This place where nature holds
the title deeds, five hours drive
away, sparkling in sub-alpine
clarity; an agnostic's perhaps
god place, all mine, all not.

How many times have I rounded
the bend into this eternal theatre,
world as was, spread before me;
then and before then, and longer ago,
and even before, hills and hills to
the horizon? How many times have
I entered this serenity, heard this
resounding clamour of silence?

Themeda, you museum of memories:
here I am, splashed by the Milky
Way, sitting in the gods, watching
wispy vapours consume all that's
familiar, and sheet-lightning revealing
nature's oldest, youngest backdrops,
and eagles sailing down the valley. How
many times Themeda, have I hiked
silent through the pines, banqueted
on nuts and cheese atop Black Hill?

Themeda, will I visit again, now
that you've been sold? Might you
be obscured by pizza delicious, or
damask and shiny goblets? So thank
you, on this, perhaps my last, here with
grandsons roaming, you showered
me with all your gifts. Perhaps in
later life, those boys, they'll be assailed
by secret voices calling them to climb
a pass, slide past plantations, so round
a bend, on their own silent eternity.

* *Themeda Rondavels, in the Mpumulanga Drakensburg near Pilgrims
Rest, our 'primitive' family haven forsomething like thirty years.*

Kite

I'm designing a kite for
those I'll never see again.
It's for healing and forgiving,
for understanding; for saying
thanks and I'm sorry. How
do I colour regret? What
shapes happiness
and love?

And when it's ready, of
hues vermilion, magenta and
saffron, singing with a hundred
voices, familiar and forgotten, so
splendidly flightworthy, the skybound
equivalent of a Viking's funerary
Longship, I'll take it to the windy
tip of Langermann Kop ; that
place overlooking half the world.

Sensing the breeze, those
obsessions will implore their
freedom. I'll play them, play them out.
We'll vibrate for a moment, they'll
strain. Resolutely, I'll let go; watch
them lifting, sailing, soaring,
smaller, smaller.

All over the world, people will
shiver with sudden, unbidden
memories.

Secret

Same bed for forty years.
Same words a thousand
times uttered. Same jokes,
same laughter. Fights that
end in a draw. Kisses, an
infinity of kisses. There's
something special here,
something precious,
something beyond
something. Is there
a secret? Yes, yes,
a secret.

Black

If, in a dim, dark space,
this were a black-framed
art-work, it would depict
a helpless black figure, fleeing
happiness across a mighty black
landscape; black trees, black fruit,
black mountains. Only the river
runs wine-green, bleeding in the
darkness, flowing from whence
to wither? no one knows! Is that
the flash of the one white paw
of the black dog tracking the
black-bound figure? And also
the sound is black, also the
bread, as is the heart today,
as is the soul.

Little Souls

Even minor artists
suffer from melancholia.
Not the despair of the mighty,
no heroic heartsore, just
minor despondencies,
whimpering away,
in little souls, at an
unvarnished table,
somewhere in
a smelly
suburb.

Advance

The line of advance is thinning.
My comrades are dropping. An
explosive flowering carries them
away; a desperate bullet; a hiccuping
pump; a vessel bursting its bounds.
The churches are harvesting my
friends. None are exempt from
half-sung hymns and palmed off
psalms.

We the skirmishing temporaries,
nurse our slowing with black
fortitude and boozy black lunches.
Some rush to kiss the cross,
while others remain darkly
objectionable.

Emerging from a myth-sheltered
life, we eye the battlefield with
distaste. There's no escape; this
is our Ypres, our Alamein. Every
morning it's over-the-top. With
patched equipment, we advance
under a Casino of shell-fire.

Top Billing

Our home is mildly voiced, not
Tuscan, Bushveld or Provencal.
Our home claims year upon year;
accretion rather than blank cheques.
Between our walls a designer might
discover apoplexy, sinking to our
favourite tatty chair surrounded by
our life time: travels and gambles
and bargains and swindles and shit
we just love. The furniture doesn't
match and the art, oh yes, the art,
the etchings claimed from dust, what
would they fetch at auction, what?
Indeed, we haven't the slightest
idea. We're comfortable here on
top of our hill, and Top Billing
is unlikely to call.

Dancing in the Dark

Ah cherie, you scandalous old
womaniser. I suppose it was
your eye for the fair sex?
Enchanted, weren't you ?
"Beautiful," you exclaimed,
"gracile," you sighed.
You showed my pristine
features to the world. At
first, you wouldn't let
another man near me.

Ah Robert, my strange old
lover. How did I fall for you,
you with your hairless face and
great staring eyes, with your
black fur flapping about your
pale skin? Ah yes, that's what
they say about older men.
Perhaps it was your hands, your
touch, never less than a caress,
often a great deal more you
old devil. Scientist indeed, it
was lust! You craved me, used
dynamite to reach me.

How we danced the night away.
You, who'd been to Paris, London,
Manhattan, saying you'd never seen
anything like it. But your flares died
so quickly, you didn't appreciate the half of it.
Oh yes, I ran the most elegant ballroom

in the hemisphere, perhaps the world.
Michelangelo indeed, God himself
decorated mine.

How I cherished those tense,
snappy steps you took, so your
torch could fall on my magnificent
features. And you'd sigh Robert, tears
would spill down your cheeks. You'd
almost given up, hadn't you?

Remember our last dances? Always
Goodnight Sweetheart; cheek to cheek we clung,
twirling, twirling on the edge of my underground lake.
Ah Robert, even after so many thousands of
years, we knew we were made for each other.
You called me Mrs Ples, but I always knew
who was the real Mrs Broom.

Eating an Olive

Eating an olive is such a
small thing; one tiny swallow,
more pit than flesh. Who decided
to pickle that bitter green fruit? Who
first pressed its oil? Was it Achilles
the goatherd, and how did he reward
Olivia, his smart wife? Olives get around:
Homer said they helped his memory;
Cleopatra placed her stones in jade;
Caesar shipped barrels full to Britain;
Hannibal's elephants couldn't get
enough. Eating an olive is no small
thing; ingest the brine of the Inland
Sea, imbibe millenia five of history.

Visitation

Mother, on our walk in
the park the other day, I
saw you smiling from your
great grandson's face.
You were there for an instant,
then gone; a fleeting manifestation
through three generations. It was
wonderful to see you, so unexpected;
isn't genetics something now?
I'll be closely watching Thomas
for your next visit.

Stories I'd like to read...

At night, tucked up in bed, I'd like
to read a story about a hi-jacked
airliner plunging into the World
Trade Centre. Wouldn't that be
audacious? I'd read it again and again.
I'd like to read a story about the
stench of thousands of unrecovered
corpses. Wouldn't that be powerful?
I'd like to read about infidels, crusades
and holy wars. Wouldn't that be romantic?
I'd like to read about the pinpoint bombing
of women and children. Wouldn't that be
too, too terribly regrettable? I'd like to read
a story of revenge and glory; of jets blazing
free from carrier decks, of tribesmen
executing everything that breathes.
Wouldn't that be heroic? I'd like to feel
the thrill of war as I drink my milk, turn
off the light. I'd like to dream about a man
making a fortune on armament shares.
Wouldn't that be capital?

Stories I'd like to read...

i wish sometimes that
my children would ask me questions
no not what is the moon made of daddy
or why do people have different coloured skins
but how has your life evolved dad
what might you have done differently
have you any regrets

did you ever meet god
how much do you love our mother
what was marvelous
but they're too busy answering their children's questions
facing their own challenges
and living the life
their children won't ask them about either

Doing Business

You know he's out there.
In the early morning silence, you
can hear him panting. You know
where he drinks and you can picture
that magnificent pair of horns he
carries. His go-away birds say he's
in Zurich or that meetings prevent
him from talking; yes all day! You
can envisage the moisture filming
his eyeballs, the cock of his head,
and the nostrils, quivering with his
peculiar shrewdness. You wonder
whether he crushes or ignores the
flies on his cheeks when showing
guests around Kruger? When four
stalkings, four misses tell the story,
you realise you'll not get within range.
You pick up the scent of a wart-hog.

Dawn is the worst. In the early
morning, you catch the slow, slick, click
of the bolt. Occasionally you glimpse a
shadow among the trees on the other
side of the water-hole. The soft-eyed cows
sense him immediately. You hear them
saying you're in London while you sign
another contract with your onyx and gold
Waterman. You note his tension as he
picks up your scent again. Deadstill,
deadstill, not a blink, not a sound, not a
flicker, and he blunders on. At a company

celebration you hear that he's collared a colleague; then you smile, arch your neck, and canter lightly away.

Canoeist

A misty, leaden,
reed-rimmed silence
seduces our expectant eyes.
Suddenly, a self-conjuring revelation
from damp air; sinister presence
hunched over its aqueous twin.

Now you see me, you dare not
glance away. But I've been here
since the beginning of time. Nothing
rare about me.

Black cloak slung about my
shoulders, I contemplate you
unblinking; but I prefer frogs.
I know what I am even if you
don't. Let me help. Just like that
I'm in the air; strong, sure, steady
on course, noble canoeist of the
sky. You may note my insignia,
undercarriage uptucked. Found
me in the book yet? No, not Purple;
do I hear someone say Goliath?
Listen to her! I settle, gluing
myself to the reeds. That's the
last clue I'm prepared to offer.

View from JAG*

bodies flat
hands up
who will be a Henry
Henry Moore
reclining anonymous
blank features
stonecast prospects

mouths gaping
hands up
who will be a William
William Kentridge corpse
gently starving [click]
gently disintegrating [jerk]
fading into landscape [click]

backs hunched
hands up
who will be a Gerard
Gerard Sekoto squatter
sniffing glue
raiding bins
dribbling poverty's perfume

lips apart
hands up
who will be a Thabo
Thabo Zuma portrait photo
smiling in the squalor
munching an apple
boarding a taxi to paradise

* *Johannesburg Art Gallery*

Collapse

Yesterday I feared the
collapse of Johannesburg.

Hyde Park staggered and
dropped to its knees under
a burden of luxury.

Northern roads were immobilised
by the press of Mercedes, Volvos
and Landrovers.

Sandton City's heart fibrillated
under a constriction of
credit cards.

Everywhere the beatification
of Capitalism; prostrating us
with envy, poor, plodding,
overdraft animals, we.

Only the cranes keep our hopes
alive; placing one storey above
another, before moving on.

But

Without memory, I'd see
things as they are. I'd allow
the Wright brothers to beget an
Airbus. Something in me wouldn't
cringe and carp. But something
mouldering remembers cleaner,
remembers gentler, remembers safer.
But, – Carl Gustav, you know this – recollection
is selective. My memories inhabit Jurrasic Park,
but I'm the dinosaur, not the blonde. I shelter
in museums and galleries, and when I drive
home, the light has changed, the colours
are otherworldly. I should be thankful,
History's allowed me two lives. But,
– Jesus, you know this – resurrection
is an article of faith.

Once

Once, I deemed myself
pristine. Now I realise, I'm
a bag of borrowed bits:
from the reptiles a little
laziness; from the mammals,
Playboy under my shirts.
Sometimes I wonder about
the crayfish of me?

Once, I thought myself
original. Now I realise, I'm
a stew of third-hand thoughts;
fashion's mannikin, rummaging
through libraries for sparks
and revelations, flossing my
general knowledge in dentist's
waiting rooms, serving
life in TV central.

Once, I admired my cool,
cool, cool. Now I'm all
a-startle. Death limps by.
I'm an amphora of anxieties;
balance-sheeting my body's
every tremour, watching
the street like a hawk, flirting
with men in black and orange.

When I met the Buddhists,
they told me I wasn't. Ergo,
there is no Ego! Life's dream

they opined, so fat with
importance, proceeds
to nothing much, and then
to dust. It's a story that
will never sell.

Junction

Who's this flashing
past the window in
war paint?
Who's this in cap
and gown?
Who's this cutting
the cake?
Who's this climbing
on my chest?
What's this railway
junction on
my face?

April

April is the noisy month;
of picnics amidst dead
leaves, mornings creaking,
murmuring toward frost.
When the last little rain
beats and grapes clamour
to ferment.

April is the silent month,
pacifying fiery light and
heat. A time of adapting
to shadows before
hunching small
for winter.

Love becomes

The passing years are chisels.
Our pretensions lie in small heaps.
A rotund figure occupies the kitchen,
while another overlords the TV kingdom.
Slowly we become visible, but even
then, it's wise to narrow our eyes.
We love and mourn and wonder.
We cease our manipulations.
One day we realise it's as though
it were arranged; chosen by some
unseen, providential hand.

Call it anything

Call it talent,
a calling, career,
earning a living.
Call it anything you like!
Some anythings I find difficult to understand.
As the man who spent seventeen years studying
dung beetles. He discovered how they orient
themselves; made a significant contribution to
scientific knowledge. Seventeen years, and it's
far from over. And then there's the woman who
exists to sprint one hundred metres at top speed.
Her life's focus lasts less than ten seconds.
Some men descend kilometres into the earth to
hew rock; a ton of rock yields an ounce of gold.
And rock bursts and underground conflagrations
and separation from their families. Let's not forget
the daft dedicates who write poetry; read by a handful,
appreciated by a fingerful, paying nothing, gleaning
them scant recognition. But poets can no more help
themselves than the dung beetle man, or the prance
prance high jumper, or those who get paid to listen
all day to human woes.

Clearing House

The books, four hundred
Rand the lot. But these are
rare Africana. What? OK, five
hundred the lot. I'll keep
these back. Right, two-fifty.
Three. Two seventy five...

Hey, be careful with that
cabinet! Oh, let's go inside
Laura. Shall we nod farewell
to the German desk Dad
bought for forty rand?
He said it'd be worth a
fortune one day. God
it's ugly!

These ornaments and glasses
Laura, with which she'd never
part! Sell them? Over my dead
body, she told Dad. Twelve
etchings, spaced so well
across the wall; see, they've
left phantoms. This stoneware
vase, so very African, made in
Edinburgh. Remember that
holiday Laura? How late one
night we played tomato-squash
at the bus stop on Princes St.
Mom and Dad shrieking like
adolescents. Do you want this
Laura? Not your style? Not for
us either.

There they go, Laura, off to
auction houses, the water
wheels of death and departure.
Wedgewood and Moorcroft,
a small Afghan, off to nurture
the cycle of life. I'm joking
Laura, I'm joking.

Will we remember Laura, on
their deathdays, when we light
candles; will we remember the
colour of the lounge furniture,
whether the dining table was
oak or stinkwood? Will we
wonder what purpose the
books? Will we love them
for the décor?

Dinner Party

Hijacks and gills with
the highballs. The renaissance
that fits and starts in Sandton
Square. The sit-tight, take-flight,
tough times in Bondi and Clapham.
It's over we artichoke,
it's over, all over, klaar, kaput,
finito. God save Africa, brave us
in Africa, with tracking devices
on our petit-four by fours for
Africa.

Complementing the carving,
the saucerers apprentice;
Mbeki's enigma variations,
the incompetence cacophony,
the corruption crescendo.
Then the fruit salad, glistening
with plums, and the just-desserts
wine, think some,
silently.

Round Three with Pietersen

We stand at the memorial.
This is our third visit.
Dead Hector hits Cecily again.
She tries not to cry.
'I always cry,' she sniffs.

We enter the museum.
Children rise up and hit us.
Marching children hit us again.
Voices we didn't hear then,
prise open our ears.
We ascend the ramp ducking and weaving.
We wonder whether that cop who fired the first shot…?
Waiting at the top of the ramp
dead Hector hits us again.
We flinch as the Green Car turns the
corner behind us.
We watch the news the world watched then.
We were so smug.

We leave, tearful and punch drunk,
off to huddle in our corner.

Old Husband

is he there
he looks substantial
enjoys three meals a day
and tidbits
no trouble with beer and wine
he farts and belches a lot
he finds TV boring
can't finish a book
the paper takes ten minutes
says he's tired of the world's bullshit
knows all the answers
dab hand at indignation
sees corruption everywhere

he seldom listens
insists it's his deafness
doesn't talk much either
how we talked when we were young
thesedays, decisions don't come easy
he's forgetful
can only do one thing at a time
mostly he's irritating
he follows instructions badly
needs constant supervision
sometimes I think he goes out of his way…

his driving leaves much to be desired
always taking the scenic route
always cursing taxi drivers
and other cowboys

he remains pigheaded
stubbornly himself
mostly concerned with
his peculiar mental life

others think he's marvelous ... marvelous
they should only know.

Hustler

When I'm home and dry
and dull, I'll picture his
opportunistic eye, blue-bright
as life, in that city of mosques
lining the sea. He'll join Sao Paulo's
muggers, up and opportune and
at me, while Zanzibar's Imams call
the faithful and the old Stone Town
falls down around. Cochin's fishermen
plunge their Chinese nets into the
rising salt. Nairobi's boiling traffic
grinds to yet another halt.

Coursing the coincidental
world, you click a life and
go. I'll add old harbour
handsome here, bustling,
happy in the photo, hustling
us onto his wondrous tub,
waving as we leave, smiling
as we hit, the first Bosphoric
lurch and heave

For Don

Here you stand
slim black rod
looking as old as your hat
dressed for Royal Ascot
and a chilly morning
it could be anywhere
but it's the land under your feet
you belong here
one of the crags

Shame

In these negotiatory times,
these times of brinkmanship blood,
I don drab clothes to explore
my confusion: dull shoes,
all-enveloping coat, wide-brimmed
hat cross-hatching my face.

Trudging sombre ways I
study my fellows who seem
to be going about their business
normally enough. A bomb here, two
or three pitched from a moving train
this morning, a burst of taxi violence.
A man complaining about the theft of
his eighty thousand rand Rolex.

Suddenly my flooding shame
floats my hat away and I'm
there for all to see.

Something yet to come

There is only this green asparagus
tip dipped in this butter, only this
yawn. There is nothing yet to come.
Only this coffee with friends, the
coffee that tastes like coffee, only
this waft of ripe peaches, only this
talking tongue. There is no medal,
there is no prize, no someplace else,
no someone else. There is only this
smile, this kiss, this hug, this joy,
this sense of loss. There is only
now, now, this hiccup of now,
there is nothing yet to come.

Homage to Donna Leon

Grand arrival, limping in an
ancient vehicle with leaks and
punctures. Our Venice was no
room at the camp grounds. Our
splendour, unlike Paola's parents,'
palazzo, was a squatter's tent on
grass near the sea. Our cherub
innocente, crawled squealing into
the Adriatic. Our Venice was the
sideways glances toilet in the
service station. We didn't glide
rondala in a gondola but, in the
vaporetto, sat next to that studious
young woman with bushy black
brows. Our darling went for the
pigeons in The Square. Was the
seven year old Commissario
Brunetti watching even then? Our
cuisine was pizza indifferente.
I promised my wife we'd return
someday to eat fancy; promises,
promises! We didn't proceed
serenely down the Grand Canal.
Harry's Bar, we visited in books.
Our Venice was being shooed by
the Carabinieri; banished too soon
from the warmth after too long in
grey chill. How we loved, how
we longed for Venice! Now,
prolific Donna keeps us posted.

Two Cabinets

Two cabinets stand in
a hallway, each aglow
with patina. Fashioned
of cured planks, from the
same tree, created both, by
the same master's hands; he
who, using eyes and ligaments
as crafty partners, coordinated
their completion within minutes.

Their feet, which tread the
earth, transmit no tremour.
Drawers slide as silk within
velvet. Doors contest the
atmosphere in closing. Not
spider's gossamer may slip
between the joints.

Their curves cause onlookers
a certain breathlessness. Their
exquisite similarities prompt
admirers to use the word,
'identical.'

When the troubles came, one
cabinet joined the chairs, while
the other, without a moment's
hesitation, fell in with the
kitchen utensils.

Road to Tonteldoos

Whither the sign to Tonteldoos,
to Nooitgedacht and Sil'kaat's
Nek; those gravelled roads, those
dust-cloud roads, the roads we
seldom take? The roads that flicker
under trees; they track the stream
and course the hills, under a smoky
moon. They'll take you to the gentlest
soul, a simple home by crystal spring,
a valley shelt'ring mastodons and
Volschenk, painting evening light.

They'll answer all life's riddles,
cleanse you under clockwork rain;
they'll offer ten resplendent birds
and many joyous years of grace.

Whither the track to Elandslaagte,
by fields and and lakes and golden
light? We know full well that magic
road, the road we seldom take.

Never

I never done nothing to you
I never
I never did
never
and I never make nobody else done
nothing to you neither
I never
I never did
and you never done nothing to me
isn't it
never
never ever
and here we are
doing nothing for one another
having nothing to do with one another
saying nothing to one another on the bus

Yeoville...

where I climbed down a drainpipe
because her parents came home early...
my father grinned and my mother
turned red

where, at the swimming baths, day after
summer's day, I honed my crawl and
primed my skin for cancer

where my lifelong addiction began,
in the smelling musky, floor polishey
and leather bound library

where, competing in my first foot race,
I choked in a hopeless cloud of dust

where, one unsuspecting night, I
found my penis, magically erect
and craving stimulation

where, coming home from school
I jumped off the moving tram
when it turned the corner from
Harrow into High

where a girl with whom I'd danced
cheek to cheek, spat at me when her
friends whispered I was not of her faith

where I hid the bicycle in the basement
from my forbidding parents

where, on the red dust field, a band of
bumblers, we soccered away the winter,
and cricketed away the summer

where, listening thro' a closed door to
raised voices, I learnt about my father's
womanising

Smiler

He materialises with the
dawn. As you wake, he's
assembling his whetstone.
How, you wonder,
can a smile be so bleak?
You represent him with
churning entrails.
You and the other victims,
are faceless, but he can
smell your blood.

He goes about his business,
cranking his whetstone,
selecting instruments.
He makes no attempt to
hide his smile.

He knows that blood
is a solvent. Today, your
blood enjoys equal rights;
yours is the democracy
of blood.

Listening to the hungry
whetstone, you wonder
why you're smiling,
pretending life
is normal?

Power Elite

Here's this old man
paying rates to the city,
with a cat on his lap,
watching TV.
An old man retired
from all importance,
noting the peripatetic
President sign a bilateral
trade agreement;
following the corrupt in
and out of court;
goggling our gymnasts
in Parliament.
Here's this once
chief executive
gathering one or two
sharp opinions for his
monthly lunch with
his old cronies when,
sitting with that grand
champion of truth,
Johnny Walker, they
reorganize the world.

Marker 12 – Forest Climbers

It wasn't the easiest
of marriages; stresses
and strains abundant.
At first I didn't feel her
soft touch, her long
kisses. Before I knew
it, we were entwined.
Lead me to the light she
crooned.

Now she stretched,
now I grew more robust.
Sumo partners, matching
heave for hold, creaking
and groaning , night and
day, offering bass to the
birdsong. Bushbucks
barked, imploring us to hush.
How she thrived with my
support.

But nothing lasts forever.
Eventually she broke it
off. Yes, she dropped
me; took my limbs crashing
to the forest floor. The hippos
screamed and fled in panic.
How bare and empty I felt.

But in that sunfilled hole,
Slowly gathering strength,
She reached out for me again.
What a woman, how can
I resist her?

Words

Some things,
words aren't good for.
Like love, and the colour
of a man's skin; those labyrinths
without exits. Using words to explain
truth, luck or evil is like leaving for Mars
by ladder. God and death shift and shiver
in a thousand kaleidoscopes. Life's enigmas
skulk in black space. Words are Mystery's comets.
They occasionally sail close. Ah, now they appear
regular, so we claim the soothing of understanding.

September

And after August's coughs and stalls,
September muscles in, all swagger hot and brassy,
hurling green grenades, trailing smoke and ash,
smelling of drains or yesterday, today and tomorrow,
eyes smarting, sneezing its head off, suddenly
showered, short sleeved, sandaled and shouting,
demanding rain, never remembering it won't
pour until the second week of October.

Memorabilia of our Time

[Christheby's conducts a millenial auction.]

One Socialist whiskers, grey and drab,
Havana Cuba.
Ten thousand pieces masonry, unauthenticated,
Berlin, Germany.
One retread, as in Magubane photo,
Soweto, South Africa.
Life of Marilyn Monroe, The Great American Novel,
Hollywood, USA.
One gas-chamber, well-organised owner, excellent condition,
Auschwitz, Poland.
Ten thousand condoms, spurned,
Durban , New York, Blantyre, Harare, etc, etc.
One war-monger, indignant, justified,
Washington, USA.
Five hundred shelves Yoricks,
Phnom Phen, Cambodia.
Picasso, five eyes, three penises,
Paris, France.
One trench, together with Waste Land,
Ypres, Belgium.
Global Village,
one skyscraper, one mud-hut.

I planned it beautiful,

envisaged it searing;
embracing the mysteries,
both tragic and comic,
passionate, anguished,
keening with hope and
redemption, a celebration
no less, of the film critics'
favourite: *the indomitable
human spirit*.
Then she married a man
named Eichmann,
to whom she bore a son.

Graveyard, Pilgrims Rest

Blue and sunny
the sky
Green and crowding
the hills
Steep and stony
the track
Sere and ragged
the plot

Blind and leaning
the headstones
Long decayed
the miners
Anonymous
their servants
Pitiful their
children
Departed too,
their mourners

No longer flash
the pans
Quiet and empty
the mines
Dug and despatched
the gold
Lonely no more
the graves
Attended now
by ghouls

Sunset at Aston Bay

Hot air balloon sun
lands behind far mountain.
The crew release rose, pink,
green, silver signals of distress,
but day joins its ancestors.
Birds flap and weep forlornly.
A shroud smudges the houses.
On go the mourning candles.
Houses are resurrected. Stars
send ancient messages of
condolence. Cars pass slowly.
The wind dies.

Evolution

No need to study fossils
or DNA mutations. No
need to read Darwin or
his disciples, St Huxley
or St Dawkins. All you
need is a dog in your lap,
or your cat. All you need
is to stroke her ribs as she
breathes. All you need is
to acknowledge the antibiotics
curing her fever. All you
need is to see the look in
her eyes as she watches
the look in yours.

Oh

oh the Pleiades
oh the Southern Cross
oh Venus in the evening and
oh, bloody approaching Mars
oh an eclipse
oh the black black holes of dark
oh the infinite reaches of our brains
oh
oh
as we thunder by on spaceship Earth

You can't place a bet on a Zebra

What
are you doing here?
How
did you get here?
What
made you come?
Not quite sure?
But, you're here, that's
the important thing.
You're welcome, but
keep still, keep quiet,
please!

What's that,
you cynical old bugger?
You can't
place a bet on a Zebra?
You can see
elephants in the zoo.
When you've seen
one sunset......
More ice
for your whiskey?
Right.

Watering hole?
No, no, not the same!
But it has a certain charm,
you'll admit.
You're beginning to
understand.

Dead twenty years, you,
the original
urban man.

So now you tell me!
We could have enjoyed
this together.
Better late than never,
eh dad?

Anniversary

Father Xmas is out of de-tox
and Christ is dead and away.
The marketers are rattling their
cups for Mothers' Day and the
aloes are in bloom, erecting their
reds and yellows in the blue of
May. Our wheel of life spins
faster as we anticipate another
celebration. Ah yes, she spots
the reds and yellows; here she
comes, and he with his glowing
purple chest, completes the
formation. For a week or two
we'll watch them, quivering
from yellow to red and back
and forth, busy with their milking
scimitars. Too soon the flowers
will dry; the sunbird pair will fly.
Where do they live? Where do
they go? Will next be the year
we'll not enjoy their autumnal
show?

Womens' Prison*

There is no peace in this peace
our defiance drumbeats every wall
There is no silence in this silence
our cause strums every bar
There is no solitary in this solitary
we walk with ants, we soar with doves
There is no penetration in this penetration
our pride annuls our searchers
There is no containment in this containment
only our struggle within this struggle
There is no ending in this beginning
yesterday and today, pain and pluck,
tears and triumph, today and tomorrow

* *Tuesday August 9, 2005*

Mike Alfred lives with his editorial wife in an old house on Langermann Kop in Kensington, Joburg. When his wife says, "I don't like it!" he returns without question to the keyboard. The couple believe themselves very fortunate in having their children and grandchildren living nearby in the city. This is Mike's second volume of published poetry. The first, *Life in the Suburb*, was published in 1994 by Snail Press. Mike writes about Joburg and its people and guides walking visitors around many parts of the 'old' city.

Printed in the United States
by Baker & Taylor Publisher Services